tasty
low fat
cooking

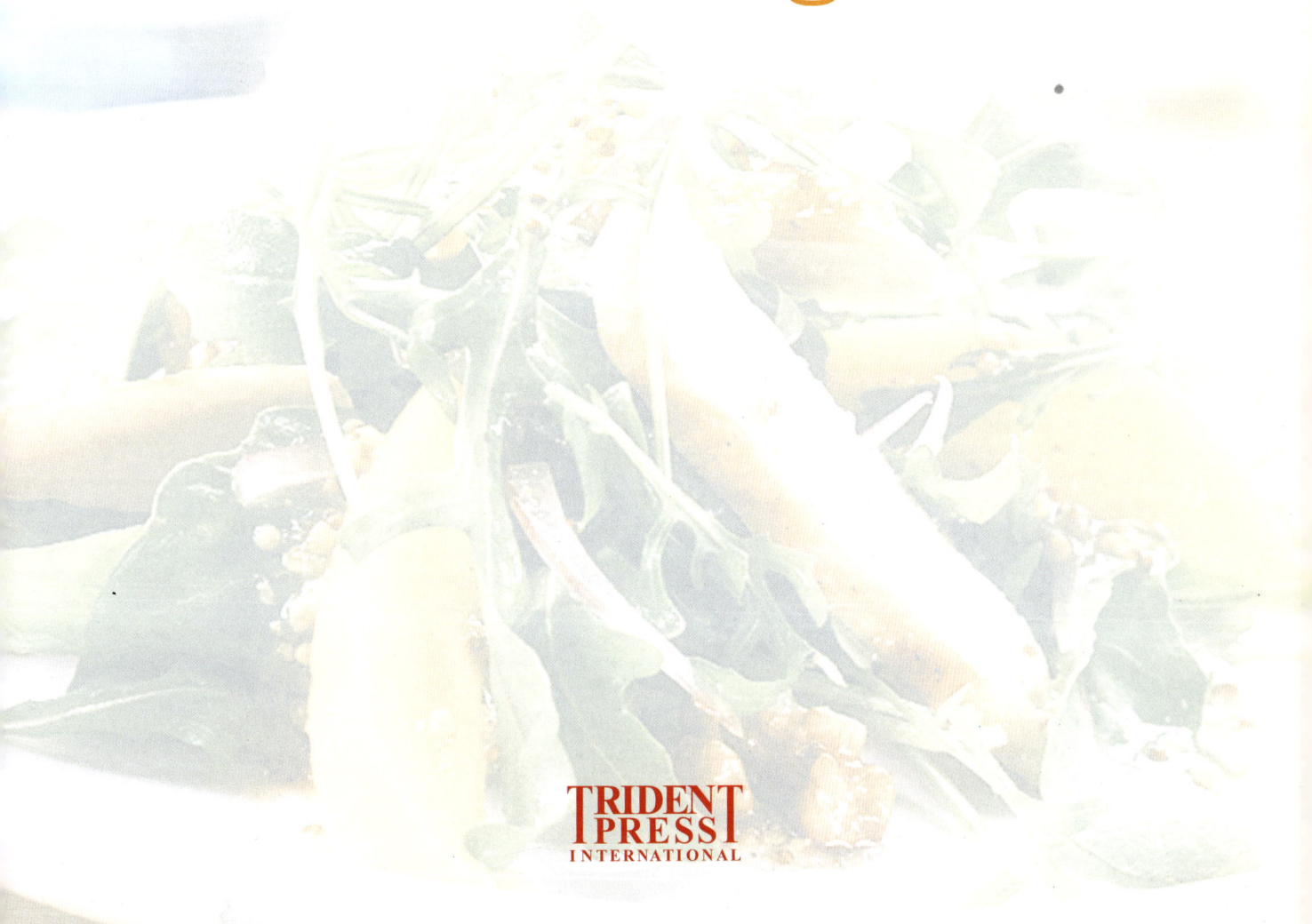

TRIDENT
PRESS
INTERNATIONAL

Published by:
TRIDENT PRESS INTERNATIONAL
801, 12th Avenue South
Suite 302
Naples, FL 34102 U.S.A.
Copyright (c)Trident Press International 2001
Tel: (941) 649 7077
Fax: (941) 649 5832
Email: tridentpress@worldnet.att.net
Website: www.trident-international.com

acknowledgements

Tasty Low Fat Cooking

Compiled by: R&R Publications Marketing Pty. Ltd.
Creative Director: Paul Sims
Production Manager: Anthony Carroll
Food Photography: Warren Webb, William Meppem,
Andre Martin, Andrew Elton, Ashley Mackevicius,
Harm Mol, Yanto Noerianto.
Food Stylists: Wendy Berecry, Rosemary De Santis,
Michelle Gorry, Donna Hay.
Recipe Development: Sheryle Eastwood, Sue Geraghty,
Anneka Mitchell, Jody Vassallo.
Proof Reader: Andrea Tarttelin

Includes Index
ISBN 1 58279097 3
EAN 9781582 790978

First Edition Printed June 2001
Computer Typeset in Humanist 521 & Times New Roman

Printed in Hong Kong

ents

introduction

be healthy, stay slim

Good food and enjoyable meals are truly one of life's great pleasures. Yet today, with the multitude of diet books and food 'scares' that regularly appear in the media, food has become a source of concern and unhappiness for many people. This book aims to counter the myths and fallacies surrounding food, dieting and nutrition. It is not just for people who are watching their weight, but also for anyone interested in healthy eating.

All recipes are low in fat, low in sugar, with no added salt. And they will give your meals a boost of all-important fibre, nature's own appetite suppressant.

Not only are they good for you and your waistline, they are also delicious, quick and easy to prepare, and suitable for all the family. When you're eating our dishes, you won't feel as if you're on a diet! Each recipe has a nutritional analysis, so you can see exactly how many kilojoules (calories), fibre, cholesterol or fat you are eating. Because weight control is more than just a diet plan, we've included information on nutrition, exercise, and body shape, latest research on obesity, eating out and help of overweight children. There is also a fat counter of common foods, as cutting down fats (including polyunsaturated fats) is currently considered the best way to stay slim and healthy. If you don't want to give up your favourite dishes, look for our tips on how to adapt recipes to be loser in fat, cholesterol and salt.

how to adapt your recipes – Limiting fat

Grill, dry-roast, stir-fry, microwave, casserole or poach in stock. A non-stick frypan or 'dry frypan' with a tight-fitting lid is a must for low-fat cookery. Also look for silicon-coated paper pan liners which line your frypan and transfer the heat to food direct - no fat needed at all!

- To brown meat or vegetables, brush your pan with oil (don't pour it in) and cook over moderate neat to avoid sticking.
- Use small quantities of butter, margarine, oil, cream, mayonnaise and cooking fats.
- Substitute low-fat dairy foods for full-cream products. Low-fat unflavoured yoghurt makes an excellent substitute for cream (do not boil after adding it). Use fat-reduced and skin milks instead of full-cream milk and ricotta, cottage cheese and fat-reduced cheeses for regular cheeses.

Reducing salt -

Don't use salt in cooking. Experiment with herbs and spices as seasoning and your palate will gradually adapt the 'real' flavour of foods, which are often masked by salt. Double quantities of garlic, onion, chilli, basil, dill, lemon juice lift the flavour.

- Slat substitutes (potassium chloride or a mixture of salt and potassium chloride) are helpful. Use low-salt und salt-free food products from the supermarket. Over 50% of sodium intake comes from commercial foods like bread, butter, margarine, cheese, ad luncheon meats which do not taste 'salty'. Stock cubes or powder, soy sauce, meat seasonings, garlic salt, Worcestershire and similar sauces all add salt.

Limiting sugar -

Gradually reduce the quantity of sugar and honey that you use.

- Offer substitutes for whipped cream for puddings - low-fat ice cream, vanilla custard, thick unflavoured yoghurt, or a blend of ricotta and yoghurt flavoured with vanilla essence and lemon rind.

Increasing fibre intake -

Where possible, do not peel vegetables, but cook with the skin on.

- Try brown rice more often. It adds an interesting nutty flavour. Try buckwheat and barley, two high-fibre grains.
- Add cooked or canned soybeans or kidney beans to casseroles; throw a handful of lentils into soups.
- For coatings or toppings use wholemeal breadcrumbs and crushed wheat biscuits (breakfast biscuits). Alternatively, try oat bran or a mixture of oat and wheat brans.

Sample recipes showing how to adapt to suit your new lifestyle

Before	*After*

Pork with **tarragon**

4 pork chops, about 200g/7 oz each
4 tablespoons plain flour
1 teaspoon salt
freshly ground black pepper
90g/3 oz butter
1 onion, chopped
$^1/_2$ cup/125ml/4fl oz dry white wine
$^1/_2$ cup/125ml/4fl oz chicken stock
1 tablespoon plain flour
1 cup/250ml/8fl oz cream
3 tablespoons fresh or 1 teaspoon dried chopped tarragon

1 *Coat pork with seasoned flour. Heat butter in a frypan and brown chops, turning each until golden in colour. Transfer to a shallow casserole dish and keep warm. Reduce heat to low.*
2 *Reduce heat in frypan to low. Add onion and cook for 2-3 minutes. Add wine and stock; pour over pork. Cover and simmer for 30 minutes or until pork is cooked.*
3 *Remove pork, Mix in flour with a little cream and tarragon. Pour sauce over pork and serve.*
Serves 4

PER SERVE		
	before	**after**
calories	263	149
kilojoules	1103	623
fat	22.5g	7g

Pork with **tarragon**

2 lean pork fillets, about 250g/8 oz each
or 4 pork medallions, fat removed
a little plain flour
freshly ground black pepper
1 tablespoon oil
1 onion, chopped
$^1/_2$ cup/125ml/4fl oz dry white wine
$^1/_2$ cup/125ml/4fl oz homemade chicken stock, without fat
2 tablespoons fresh or $^1/_2$ teaspoon dried tarragon
1 tablespoon plain flour
3 tablespoons cream
$^1/_2$ cup/125ml/4fl oz thick plain yoghurt
1 tablespoon fresh chopped tarragon (extra)

1 *Combine flour and pepper and coat pork. Place in an oiled baking dish and bake in a moderate oven 180°C/350°F for 15 minutes until just cooked.*
2 *Heat oil in a small saucepan and cook onion for 1-2 minutes or until golden. Add wine, stock and tarragon, cook for another 1-2 minutes, scraping sides of pan.*
3 *Mix flour with cream until smooth and stir into pan with yoghurt (do not boil). Keep warm until needed.*
4 *To serve, slice pork fillet and place 3-4 rounds on each plate. Spoon a little sauce over each; serve and garnish with extra tarragon.*
Serves 4

herbs
and spices

There are many flavour-packed ingredients with little or no kilojoules (calories) which you can use to improve the flavour of a dish. Garlic, lemon rind, curry powder, soy sauce are familiar examples, as well as aromatic herbs (both fresh and dried). Start using these in place of butter, cream, bacon and other high-fat ingredients, which often feature in traditional cookery. If you're cutting back on slat, herbs and spices become even more important. Fresh and pure dried herbs and spices contain virtually no sodium (salt chemically is sodium chloride), but be sure to check the label of herb mixtures. Some, such as 'celery salt', 'garlic salt' or 'herb seasoning' often contain salt as an ingredient.

Enhance the flavour of your favourite foods:

Fish - Bay leaf, chives, dill, fennel, horseradish, oregano, parsley, tarragon

Chicken, turkey - Garlic, pepper, rosemary, sage, tarragon, thyme

Beef, veal - Cumin, garlic, horseradish, marjoram, oregano, pepper, thyme

Lamb, mutton - Coriander, mint, rosemary, sorrel

Pork - Savory, ginger, caraway, paprika, garlic, sage, thyme

Vegetables - Basil, borage, caraway, chervil, chives, coriander, fennel, dill, garlic, mint, mustard, nasturtium, oregano, parsley, pepper, sage, salad burnett, savory, thyme

Eggs - Basil, caraway, chervil, chives, sage

Fruit - Allspice, aniseed, cinnamon, cloves, ginger, nutmeg, vanilla more about herbs

Fresh herbs can be dried or frozen for winter use. Basil, thyme, marjoram and nasturtium can be used as a pepper substitute. Herbs can be used to replace salt intake: try lovage, thyme and marjoram. Scatter edible flowers of borage all look fantastic used this way. Fresh herbs should be chopped only at the last moment so that the full flavour of the aromatic oils is captured in the dish. Basil and savory are a boon to people on low-salt diets. Fresh is best. Many fresh herbs such as caraway, chervil, lemon balm, salad burnet, savory and sorrel are not readily available from the local fruit and vegetable market but can all be grown easily and quickly in your garden or on the kitchen windowsill.

basil

bay leaves

 dill

caraway

 horseradish

chillies

lemon/orange rind

chinese five spice

mint

chives

 mushrooms

cinnamon

nutmeg

cloves

parsley

coriander

rosemary

puffed nut granola

start the day

It's time to consider the vitality

and goodness you gain from eating breakfast - it only takes a few minutes! A balanced breakfast keeps you going until lunch and there is less temptation to snack.

mighty
muesli

ingredients

4 cups/380g rolled oats
2 tablespoons shredded coconut
3 tablespoons oat bran
3 tablespoons wheat germ
I cup/40g oat flakes
3 tablespoons sunflower kernels
4 tablespoons chopped dried peaches
3 tablespoons chopped dried pears
3 tablespoons currants

Method:

1 *Place rolled oats and coconut in a baking dish and bake for 15-20 minutes, or until oats and coconut are toasted. Stir several times during cooking to ensure even toasting. Remove from oven and set aside to cool.*
2 *Place cooled rolled oats and coconut, oat bran, wheat germ, oat flakes, sunflower kernels, dried peaches, dried pears and currants in a bowl. Mix well to combine.*

   Serving suggestion: *Sprinkle with banana chips if desired and top with icy cold milk or juice.*

Makes 20 servings

530 kilojoules/125 calories per serve
Fat *Medium* **Fibre** *Medium*

Oven temperature 180°C, 350°F, Gas 4

puffed
nut granola

Photograph page 9

ingredients

90g/3oz puffed corn
I cup/90g/3oz rolled oats
¹/₂ cup/30g/Ioz bran cereal
90g/3oz Brazil nuts, roughly choppd
30g/Ioz flaked coconut
I teaspoon ground cinnamon
¹/₃ cup/90mL/3fl oz unsweetened apple juice
2 tablespoons honey
125g/4oz dried apricots, chopped
125g/4oz dried pears, chopped
90g/3oz pitted fresh or dried dates, chopped

Method:

1 *Place puffed corn, rolled oats, bran cereal, nuts, coconut, cinnamon, apple juice and honey in a bowl and mix well to combine.*
2 *Place mixture in a shallow ovenproof dish, spread out evenly and bake, stirring occasionally, for 20-30 minutes or until golden.*
3 *Set aside to cool slightly. Add apricots, pears and dates and toss to combine. Set aside to cool completely. Store in an airtight container.*

Serves 10

1081 kilojoules/259 calories per serve -
Fat *low* **Fibre** *high*

Oven temperature 180°C, 350°F, Gas 4

fruit
and yoghurt porridge

Method:

1. Place milk, rolled oats, apples, sultanas and cinnamon in a saucepan and mix to combine. Cook over a medium heat, stirring, for 5-7 minutes or until oats are soft. Spoon porridge into serving bowls and serve topped with a spoonful of yoghurt.

Serves 2

1600 kilojoules/382 calories per serve
Fat medium   **Fibre** high

ingredients

2 cups/500mL/16fl oz low-fat milk
³/₄ cup/75g/2¹/₂oz rolled oats
3 tablespoons chopped dried apples
3 tablespoons sultanas
1 teaspoon ground cinnamon
2 tablespoons low-fat natural
or diet fruit yoghurt

summer
fruit breakfast

Method:

1 *Place nectarines, peaches, raspberries and blueberries in a bowl and toss to combine. Divide fruit between serving bowls.*

2 *Place yogurt, wheat germ and maple syrup into a bowl and mix to combine. Spoon yoghurt mixture over fruit and serve.*
Serves 4

647 kilojoules/155 calories per serve -
***Fat** low* ***Fibre** high*

ingredients

3 nectarines, sliced
3 peaches, sliced
125g/4oz raspberries
125g/4oz blueberries
1 cup/200g/6¹/₂oz low-fat
vanilla-flavoured yoghurt
45g/1¹/₂oz wheat germ
1 tablespoon maple syrup

wholemeal
nutty pancakes

Method:

1 Place flour and sugar in a bowl and mix to combine. Add yoghurt, milk and egg and whisk to combine. Fold in blueberries and nuts.

2 Heat a nonstick frying pan over a low heat, pour 2 tablespoons of batter into pan and cook for 2 minutes or until bubbles appear on the surface. Turn pancake over and cook for 2 minutes longer or until golden on second side. Remove pancake from pan and repeat with remaining batter.

Serves 4

1909 kilojoules/456 calories per serve -
Fat medium   **Fibre** high

ingredients

1 cup/155g/5oz wholemeal
self-raising flour
1/2 cup/90g/3oz brown sugar
250g/8oz low-fat natural yoghurt
1/3 cup/90mL/3fl oz reduced-fat milk
1 egg, lightly beaten
250g/8oz blueberries
90g/3oz macadamia nuts,
roughly chopped

mixed
mushroom frittata

Method:

1 *Place eggs, milk, mustard, dill and black pepper to taste in a bowl and whisk to combine.*

2 *Heat a nonstick frying pan over a medium heat, spray with polyunsaturated cooking oil spray, add spring onions and cook, stirring, for 2 minutes. Add oyster, field and button mushrooms and cook, stirring, for 3 minutes longer or until mushrooms are tender.*

3 *Pour egg mixture into pan and cook over a low heat for 5 minutes or until frittata is almost set.*

4 *Place pan under a preheated medium grill and cook for 3 minutes or until top is golden.*

Serves 4

479 kilojoules/114 calories per serve -
Fat *low* **Fibre** *medium*

ingredients

4 eggs, lightly beaten
¹/₂ cup/125mL/4fl oz reduced-fat milk
1 tablespoon Dijon mustard
2 tablespoons chopped fresh dill
freshly ground black pepper
4 spring onions, chopped
125g/4oz oyster mushrooms
125g/4oz field mushrooms, sliced
125g/4oz button mushrooms, sliced

turkey
muffins

Method:

1 Place tomato slices on muffin halves. Top with turkey slices, cheese and black pepper to taste. Place under a preheated grill until heated through.

Serves 2

1055 kilojoules/250 calories per serve
Fat *low*   **Fibre** *medium*

ingredients

2 muffins, halved and toasted

Topping
1 tomato, sliced
2 slices cooked turkey breast
3 tablespoons grated low-fat tasty cheese
freshly ground black pepper

muesli cakes

need
a snack

Snacks aren't necessarily to blame

for a failed attempt at weight loss. When well-planned, snacks can be part of a healthy eating plan. However, remember some snacks contribute little except fat, salt and lots of unwanted kilojoules (calories)!

crispy
pizza rolls

ingredients

2 large wholemeal pitta bread rounds, split
4 tablespoons tomato paste (purée)
1/2 green capsicum (pepper), chopped
2 slices reduced-fat ham, chopped
2 spring onions, chopped
60g/2oz grated reduced-fat
Cheddar cheese

Method:
1 Spread each bread round with 1 tablespoon tomato paste (purée) leaving a 2cm/3/4in border. Sprinkle with green capsicum (pepper), ham, spring onions and cheese.
2 Roll up bread rounds and cut in half. Secure with a wooden toothpick or cocktail stick. Place rolls on baking trays and bake for 20 minutes or until bread is crisp. Serve hot or cold.

Makes 8

428 kilojoules/102 calories per roll -
Fat *low* **Fibre** *low*

Oven temperature 180°C, 350°F, Gas 4

muesli
cakes

Photograph page 17

ingredients

1 3/4 cups/280g/9oz wholemeal
self-raising flour
1/3 cup/90g/3oz sugar
75g/2 1/2oz polyunsaturated margarine,
chopped
3/4 cup/90g/3oz untoasted natural muesli
1/4 cup/45g/1 1/2oz sultanas
1/2 teaspoon mixed spice
1/2 cup/125mL/4fl oz low-fat milk
or buttermilk
1/4 cup/45g/1 1/2oz low-fat natural yoghurt
1 egg, lightly beaten

Method:
1 Place flour, sugar and margarine in a food processor and process until mixture resembles breadcrumbs.
2 Transfer flour mixture to a bowl, add muesli, sultanas, mixed spice, milk, yoghurt and egg and mix to form a soft, slightly sticky dough.
3 Take 2 tablespoons of mixture and drop onto a nonstick baking tray. Repeat with remaining mixture and bake for 15 minutes or until cakes are cooked and golden. Transfer to wire racks to cool.

Makes 20

471 kilojoules/113 calories per cake -
Fat *low* **Fibre** *medium*

Oven temperature 190°C, 375°F, Gas 5

pancake
sandwiches

Method:

1 Place flour and sugar in a bowl and mix to combine. Make a well in centre of flour mixture, add egg and milk and mix until smooth.

2 Heat a nonstick frying pan over a medium heat, drop tablespoons of batter into pan and cook for 1 minute each side or until golden. Remove pancake, set aside and keep warm. Repeat with remaining batter to make 12 pancakes.

3 To make filling, place ricotta cheese, lemon juice and sugar in a food processor or blender and process until smooth.

4 To assemble, top half the pancakes with filling, then with remaining pancakes.

Makes 6

569 kilojoules/136 calories per serve -
***Fat** low   **Fibre** low*

ingredients

³/₄ **cup/90g/3oz self-raising flour**
1 tablespoon sugar
1 egg, lightly beaten
³/₄ **cup/185mL/6fl oz low-fat milk**
or buttermilk

Lemon ricotta filling
¹/₂ **cup/125g/4oz ricotta cheese**
2 tablespoons lemon juice
1 tablespoon sugar

curried
pumpkin soup

Method:

1 Heat oil in a large saucepan. Cook onion, coriander, cumin and chilli powder until onion softens.

2 Cut pumpkin into cubes and add to saucepan with stock. Cook pumpkin for 20 minutes or until tender, then cool slightly. Transfer soup in batches to a food processor or blender and process until smooth.

3 Return soup to a rinsed saucepan and heat. Season to taste with pepper.

Serves 4

601 kilojoules/144 calories per serve
Fat low   **Fibre** medium

ingredients

1 tablespoon polyunsaturated oil
1 large onion, chopped
1/2 teaspoon ground coriander
1/2 teaspoon ground cumin
1/2 teaspoon chilli powder
1 kg/2lb pumpkin, peeled and seeds removed
4 cups/1 litre chicken stock
freshly ground black pepper

herb
and cheese loaf

Method:

1 In a bowl combine flour, rolled oats, bran, low fat and Parmesan cheeses, chives and parsley. Make a well in the centre of the dry ingredients. Add milk and oil. Mix to combine.
2 Beat egg whites until stiff peaks form. Lightly fold through dough.
3 Spoon into a 23x12cm/9x5in non-stick loaf pan. Bake at 180°C/350°F/Gas 4 for 40 minutes.

Serves 12

678 kilojoules/161 calories per serve
Fat medium   **Fibre** high

ingredients

1 ¼ cups/170g self-raising wholemeal flour
1 cup/90g rolled oats
1 cup/45g unprocessed bran
½ cup/60g grated low fat cheese
1 tablespoon grated Parmesan cheese
2 tablespoons chopped chives
2 tablespoons chopped fresh parsley
1 cup/250mL low fat milk
4 tablespoons safflower oil
3 egg whites

Oven temperature 180°C, 350°F, Gas 4

spicy rice
tomato and vegetables

Method:

1 *Heat oil in a large saucepan. Cook onion, capsicum and chilli for 3-4 minutes. Add rice, mix well and cook for 3-4 minutes.*

2 *Add tomatoes to the pan with stock or water. Bring to the boil and simmer for 30 minutes or until liquid is absorbed and rice is tender. Season with pepper.*

Serves 4

751 kilojoules/182 calories per serve

Fat *low* **Fibre** *high*

ingredients

1 tablespoon olive oil
1 onion, sliced
1 green capsicum (pepper), diced
1 red chilli, seeded and finely chopped
³/₄ cup/170g white rice
³/₄ cup/170g quick-cooking brown rice
400g/13oz canned peeled tomatoes, undrained and roughly chopped
1¹/₂ cups/375mL vegetable stock or water
freshly ground black pepper

lasagne

Method:

1 Heat oil in a frypan. Cook onion and garlic for 2-3 minutes. Add mince and cook over medium heat until well browned. Combine soy beans, tomatoes, tomato paste, 2 teaspoons basil, oregano and sugar. Drain pan of any juices and stir in tomato mixture. Simmer, uncovered, for 15 minutes or until sauce thickens slightly.

2 Spread half the meat mixture over the base of a 15x25cm/6x10in ovenproof dish. Top with three lasagne sheets, placed side by side. Repeat with remaining meat mixture and lasagne sheets.

3 Place ricotta cheese, cottage cheese and egg white in a food processor or blender and process until smooth. Spread cheese mixture over lasagne in dish. Top with Parmesan cheese and remaining basil. Bake at 200°C/400°F/Gas 6 for 35-40 minutes or until tender.

How We've Cut Fat and Kilojoules

We have used lean minced beef for the filling. We alternated a layer of vege-table with the meat to keep the fibre high and the kilojoules low.

Instead of the usual rich Bechamel cheese sauce on top, we made a lighter version based on skim milk and cornflour.

Serves 4

1091 kilojoules/262 calories per serve
Fat low **Fibre** high

ingredients

2 teaspoons olive oil
1 onion, chopped
1 clove garlic, crushed
155g/5oz lean ground beef
315g/10oz canned soy beans, drained
440g/14oz canned peeled tomatoes, undrained and mashed
1 tablespoon tomato paste
1 1/2 tablespoons chopped fresh basil
1/4 teaspoon dried oregano leaves
1/4 teaspoon sugar
6 sheets instant spinach lasagne noodles
1/2 cup/125g ricotta cheese
1/2 cup/125g cottage cheese
1 egg white
1 tablespoon grated Parmesan cheese

Oven temperature 200°C, 400°F, Gas 6

salmon in pepper and mint

keep fit with fish

Seafood is good news for slimmers.

All seafood is low in kilojoules (calories), with fewer kilojoules (calories) than even the leanest meat or chicken. And, of course, with seafood you don't need to trim any fat. Just grill, barbeque, bake, steam, poach or microwave seafood to keep a low kilojoule (calorie) count.

crispy
potatoes

ingredients

6 potatoes, scrubbed
sea salt
1 tablespoon chopped fresh rosemary

Method:

1 *Cut potatoes into wedges. Place on a very lightly greased baking tray and spray lightly with polyunsaturated cooking oil spray.*
2 *Sprinkle potatoes with salt and rosemary and bake, turning occasionally, for 35-45 minutes or until potatoes are crisp and golden.*

Serves 6

Note:

Nothing like crispy potato chips to compliment your fish dish.

Oven temperature 200°C, 400°F, Gas 6

salmon
with pepper and mint

Photograph page 25

ingredients

4 salmon cutlets

Pepper and mint marinade
3 tablespoons dry white wine
2 tablespoons lime juice
2 tablespoons chopped fresh mint
2 teaspoons crushed black peppercorns

Method:

1 *To make marinade, place wine, lime juice, mint and black pepper in a large shallow glass or ceramic dish and mix to combine.*
2 *Add salmon to marinade and set aside to marinate for 10 minutes. Turn once. Drain and cook on a preheated hot barbecue or under a grill for 2-3 minutes each side or until salmon flakes when tested with a fork. Serve immediately.*

Serves 4

903 kilojoules/216 calories per serve -
Fat *medium* **Fibre** *low*

marinated
trout fillets

Method:

1 To make marinade, place lime juice, thyme, mustard seeds, bay leaves and black pepper to taste in a shallow glass or ceramic dish.

2 Add trout fillets to marinade and set aside to marinate, turning several times, for 15 minutes. Drain trout well.

3 Heat a nonstick frying pan over a medium heat. Add trout and cook for 2-3 minutes each side or until fish flakes when tested with fork. Serve immediately.

Serves 6

1355 kilojouies/324 calories per serve -
***Fat** low*   ***Fibre** low*

ingredients

12 small trout fillets

Lime and thyme marinade
2 tablespoons lime juice
2 tablespoons fresh lemon thyme or thyme or 1 teaspoon dried thyme
1 tablespoon yellow mustard seeds
2 bay leaves
freshly ground black pepper

keep fit
with fish

spiced
fish kebabs

Method:

1 *Thread fish onto lightly oiled skewers. Place paprika, black pepper, cumin and chilli powder in a bowl and mix to combine. Sprinkle spice mixture over kebabs.*

2 *Cook kebabs under a preheated hot grill or on a barbecue for 2-3 minutes each side or until fish is cooked.*

3 *To make sauce, place yoghurt, lemon juice, thyme and black pepper to taste in a bowl and mix to combine. Serve with kebabs.*

Serves 4

1011 kilojoules/242 calories per serve - **Fat** *medium* **Fibre** *low*

ingredients

750g/1 1/2 lb firm white fish fillets, cut into 2 1/2cm/1in cubes
1 tablespoon ground paprika
2 teaspoons crushed black peppercorns
1 teaspoon ground cumin
1/2 teaspoon chilli powder

Lemon yoghurt sauce
1/2 cup/100g/3 1/2oz low-fat natural yoghurt
1 tablespoon lemon juice
1 tablespoon chopped fresh lemon thyme or 1/2 teaspoon dried thyme
freshly ground black pepper

fish cutlets
with italian sauce

Method:

1 Brush fish cutlets with lemon juice. Place under a preheated griller and cook for 4-5 minutes each side. Remove from griller and keep warm.

2 Place shallots, garlic, tomatoes, mushrooms, wine, basil, oregano and pepper to taste in a saucepan. Bring to the boil. Reduce heat and simmer gently for 8-10 minutes.

3 Arrange fish cutlets on serving plates. Spoon sauce over and top with Parmesan cheese.

Serves 4

876 kilojoules/206 calories per serve
Fat low   **Sodium** medium

ingredients

4x150g/5oz white fish cutlets
2 tablespoons lemon juice
6 shallots, finely chopped
1 clove garlic, crushed
400g/13oz canned tomatoes (no added salt)
200g/6¹/₂oz button mushrooms, sliced
¹/₂ cup/125mL red wine
2 teaspoons finely chopped fresh basil
¹/₂ teaspoon dried oregano
freshly ground black pepper
2 tablespoons grated Parmesan cheese

salmon
souffles

Method:

1 Combine salmon, oysters, capers, dill, Tabasco and cottage cheese in a bowl. Season to taste with pepper.

2 Beat egg whites until stiff peaks form and fold lightly through salmon mixture. Spoon into four lightly greased individual soufflé dishes and bake at 200°C/400°F/Gas 6 for 30-35 minutes.

Serves 4

550 kilojoules/132 calories per serve
Fat low   **Fibre** low

ingredients

220g/7oz canned red salmon, no-added-salt, drained and flaked
100g/3¹/₂oz bottled oysters, drained, rinsed and chopped
2 teaspoons finely chopped capers
1 teaspoon finely chopped fresh dill
2-3 dashes Tabasco sauce
1 cup/250g low fat cottage cheese
freshly ground black pepper
4 egg whites

teriyaki
fish

Method:

1 Place fish fillets in a single layer in a shallow dish. To make marinade, combine teriyaki sauce, honey, sherry, ginger and garlic and pour over fish. Cover and marinate for 1 hour.

2 Toss sesame seeds in a frypan and cook over medium heat until golden brown, stirring frequently.

3 Remove fish from marinade and grill for 2-3 minutes, each side. Baste occasionally with marinade during cooking. Serve sprinkled with sesame seeds.

Serves 4

1140 kilojoules/270 calories per serve
Fat low   **Fibre** low

ingredients

4 large white fish fillets
2 teaspoons sesame seeds

Marinade
3 tablespoons teriyaki sauce
1 tablespoon honey
1 tablespoon dry sherry
$^1/_4$ teaspoon grated fresh ginger
1 clove garlic, crushed

**keep fit
with fish**

lemon
fish parcels

Method:

1 *Lightly grease four sheets of aluminium foil and place a fish fillet in the centre of each sheet.*

2 *Top each fillet with a teaspoon of capers. Pour over lemon juice and season with pepper. Place two asparagus spears over each fillet and dust lightly with paprika.*

3 *Fold up edges of aluminium foil and completely encase fish. Place parcels on an oven tray and bake at 180°C/350°F/Gas 4 for 15-20 minutes, or until fish flakes when tested with a fork. Remove from parcels to serve.*

Serves 4

526 kilojoules/125 calories per serve
Fat *low* **Fibre** *low*

ingredients

4 large white fish fillets
1 tablespoon finely chopped capers
$1/2$ cup/125mL lemon juice
freshly ground black pepper
8 asparagus spears (fresh or canned)
$1/2$ teaspoon paprika

Oven temperature 180°C, 350°F, Gas 4

steamed
spiced fish with nuts

Method:

1 Pat fish dry with absorbent kitchen paper and set aside.

2 Place coriander, chives, garlic, ginger, cumin, paprika, turmeric, cayenne pepper and lime juice in a shallow glass or ceramic dish and mix to combine. Add fish, cover and marinate in the refrigerator for 2 hours.

3 Cut four circles of aluminium foil large enough to completely enclose the fillets. The foil should be at least 10cm/4in larger than the fillets on all sides. Fold foil in half lengthwise and cut a half-heart shape. Open out foil.

4 Place a fillet on one half of each foil heart, near the centre line, then sprinkle with pistachio nuts. Fold foil over fish and roll edges to seal. Place parcels on a rack set in a baking dish. Add ½ cup/125mL/4fl oz hot water to baking dish and bake for 15 minutes or until fish flakes when tested with a fork.

Serves 4

1210 kilojoules/289 calories per serve - **Fat** *medium* **Fibre** *medium*

ingredients

4 firm white fish fillets
2 tablespoons chopped fresh coriander
2 tablespoons snipped fresh chives
2 cloves garlic, crushed
2½cm/1in piece fresh ginger, finely chopped
2 teaspoons ground cumin
2 teaspoons paprika
1 teaspoon ground turmeric
¼ teaspoon cayenne pepper
2 tablespoons lime juice
90g/3oz pistachio nuts, toasted and roughly chopped

chicken mango pockets

it's lunch

With the exception of breakfast,

lunch is the meal most often missed. It is, however, the pitstop most needed to get you through the daily trauma of work at the office or at home. It also stops the snack attack which, if one succumbs,can result in a diet blow-out.

layered
lunch loaf

ingredients

1 round rye or wholegrain cottage loaf

Mixed sprouts layer
2 teaspoons tomato paste (purée)
4 tablespoons low-fat natural yoghurt
1 teaspoon ground cilantra (coriander)
90g/3oz alfalfa sprouts
60g/2oz bean sprouts
**90g/3oz snow pea (mangetout) sprouts
or watercress**

Roast beef layer
3 teaspoons French mustard
4 slices lean rare roast beef
4 lettuce leaves of your choice
1/2 red capsicum (pepper), chopped

Tomato salad layer
2 tomatoes, sliced
3 gherkins, sliced
1/2 cucumber, sliced

Method:
1 *Cut bread horizontally into four even layers.*
2 *For sprouts layer, place tomato paste (purée), yoghurt and coriander in a bowl and mix to combine. Place alfalfa sprouts, bean sprouts and snow pea (mangetout) sprouts or watercress on bottom layer of bread. Top with yoghurt mixture and second bread layer.*
3 *For beef layer, spread bread with mustard, then top with roast beef, lettuce and red pepper (capsicum) and third bread layer.*
4 *For salad layer, top bread with tomatoes, gherkins and cucumber and final bread layer. Serve cut into wedges.*
Serves 4

1433 kilojoules/342 calories per serve -
Fat *low* **Fibre** *high*

chicken
mango pockets

ingredients

4 wholemeal pitta bread rounds
90g/3oz ricotta cheese
1 small cucumber, chopped
2 tablespoons chopped fresh mint
1 teaspoon ground cumin
1 red onion, thinly sliced
90g/3oz alfalfa sprouts
**500g/1 lb cooked chicken, skin
removed and flesh shredded**
4 tablespoons mango chutney

Method:
1 *Make a slit in the top of each pitta bread round. Set aside.*
2 *Place ricotta cheese, cucumber, mint and cumin in a bowl and mix to combine. Spread the inside of each pitta bread with ricotta mixture, then fill with onion, alfalfa sprouts, chicken and chutney.*
Serves 4

1880 kilojoules/449 calories per serve - **Fat** *medium* **Fibre** *medium*

Photograph page 35

greek
tuna focaccia

Method:

1 Split focaccia bread horizontally and toast lightly under a preheated medium grill.
2 Top each piece of bread with feta cheese, rocket or watercress, tuna, sun-dried tomatoes, capers and onion rings. Sprinkle with dill.

Serves 4

1864 kilojoules/445 calories per serve -
Fat *low*   **Fibre** *high*

ingredients

2x10cm/4in squares focaccia bread
90g/3oz marinated or plain feta cheese, crumbled
¹/₂ bunch rocket or watercress, broken into sprigs
440g/14oz canned tuna in brine or springwater, drained
60g/2oz sun-dried tomatoes in oil, drained and sliced
1 tablespoon capers, drained
1 onion, thinly sliced into rings
1 tablespoon chopped fresh dill

chicken
and asparagus rolls

Method:

1 Boil, steam or microwave asparagus until just tender. Drain and set aside to cool.
2 Place chicken and chutney in a bowl and mix to combine. Top pitta bread with chicken mixture, asparagus, cucumber and green capsicum (pepper). Roll up.

Serves 2

1948 kilojoules/465 calories per roll -
Fat *medium* **Fibre** *high*

ingredients

250g/8oz asparagus spears
**125g/4oz chopped cooked chicken, all
skin and visible fat removed**
1 tablespoon tomato chutney
2 large wholemeal pitta bread rounds
¹/₂ cucumber, sliced
¹/₂ green capsicum (pepper), sliced

grilled
ricotta focaccia

Method:

1 Spread each piece of focaccia bread with mustard, then top with tomatoes, green capsicum (pepper) and mushrooms.

2 Place ricotta cheese, rosemary and black pepper to taste in a bowl and mix to combine. Top vegetable mixture with ricotta mixture and cook under a preheated hot grill for 3 minutes or until heated through and slightly brown.

Serves 2

1486 kilojoules/355 calories per serve -
Fat *medium* **Fibre** *high*

ingredients

2x12¹/₂cm/5in squares focaccia bread,
split and toasted
2 tablespoons wholegrain mustard
2 tomatoes, sliced
¹/₂ green capsicum (pepper), sliced
4 mushrooms, sliced
4 tablespoons ricotta cheese
2 teaspoons chopped fresh rosemary
freshly ground black pepper

roasted
garlic and tomato soup

Photograph page 41

Method:

1 Place tomatoes and garlic in a lightly greased shallow ovenproof dish, brush lightly with oil and sprinkle with salt and black pepper to taste. Bake for 30 minutes or until garlic is golden and tomatoes are soft. Cool slightly.

2 Place tomatoes, garlic and stock in batches into food processor or blender and process until smooth.

3 Place soup mixture and onion in a saucepan, bring to simmering and simmer for 10 minutes or until heated through. Stir in basil and serve.

Serves 6

295 kilojoules/71 calories per serve -
Fat *low* **Fibre** *medium*

ingredients

1 kg/2 lb plum (egg or Italian) tomatoes, halved
5 cloves garlic, peeled
1 tablespoon olive oil
sea salt
freshly ground black pepper
6 cups/1½ litres/2½pt vegetable stock
1 large red onion, finely chopped
3 tablespoons chopped fresh basil

Oven temperature 190°C, 375°F, Gas 5

leek
and parsnip soup

Photograph page 41

Method:

1 Heat oil and butter in a saucepan over a medium heat, add leeks and cook for 5 minutes or until leeks are golden.

2 Add parsnips, orange rind and 1 cup/250mL/ 8fl oz stock to pan, cover, cook over a low heat for 15 minutes or until parsnips are soft.

3 Stir in remaining stock, water and black pepper to taste, bring to simmering and simmer for 30 minutes longer. Remove pan from heat and set aside to cool slightly.

4 Place soup in batches into food processor or blender and process until smooth. Return soup to a clean pan, bring to simmering and simmer for 5 minutes or until heated through. Sprinkle with chives and serve.

Serves 6

590 kilojoules/141 calories per serve -
Fat *low* **Fibre** *medium*

ingredients

1 tablespoon olive oil
30g/1oz butter
2 leeks, sliced
750g/1½lb parsnips, peeled and sliced
1 teaspoon finely grated orange rind
4 cups/1 litre/1¾pt chicken stock
2 cups/500mL/16fl oz water
freshly ground black pepper
2 tablespoons snipped fresh chives

pesto
potato salad

Photograph page 43

ingredients

10 small potatoes, chopped
2 spring onions, chopped

Pesto dressing
1/3 cup/60g/2oz low-fat natural yoghurt
4 tablespoons chopped fresh basil
2 tablespoons grated Parmesan cheese
1 clove garlic, crushed
freshly ground black pepper

Method:
1 Boil, steam or microwave potatoes until tender. Drain and set aside to cool.
2 To make dressing, place yoghurt, basil, Parmesan cheese, garlic and black pepper to taste in a food processor or blender and process to combine.
3 Place potatoes and spring onions in a bowl. Spoon over dressing and toss to combine. Cover and refrigerate until required.
Serves 4

565 kilojoules/135 calories per serve -
Fat *low* **Fibre** *medium*

lebanese
salad

Photograph page 43

ingredients

1/3 cup/60g/2oz burghul (cracked wheat)
125g/4oz canned chickpeas, rinsed and drained
2 tomatoes, chopped
1/2 bunch fresh parsley, chopped
3 tablespoons chopped fresh mint
1 1/2 tablespoons lemon juice
freshly ground black pepper
wholemeal flatbread

Creamy chickpea dressing
3 tablespoons hummus
3 tablespoons low-fat natural yoghurt
1/2 teaspoon chilli powder
1/2 teaspoon ground cumin

Method:
1 Place burghul (cracked wheat) in a bowl, cover with boiling water and set aside to stand for 10-15 minutes or until soft. Drain.
2 Place burghul (cracked wheat), chickpeas, tomatoes, parsley, mint, lemon juice and black pepper to taste in a bowl and toss to combine.
3 To make dressing, place hummus, yoghurt, chilli powder and cumin in a bowl and mix to combine. Spoon dressing over salad and pack into containers. Serve with flat bread.
Note: *If canned chickpeas are unavailable, use cold cooked chickpeas instead. To cook chickpeas, soak overnight in cold water. Drain. Place in a saucepan, cover with cold water and bring to the boil over a medium heat. Boil for 10 minutes, then reduce heat and simmer for 45-60 minutes or until chickpeas are tender. Drain and cool. Cooked chickpeas freeze well, so cook more than you need and freeze what you do not use.*
Serves 2

1192 kilojoules/285 Calories per serve -
Fat *medium to high* **Fibre** *high*

steamed
ginger chilli mussels

Method:

1 To make sauce, place ginger, garlic, lemon grass, chillies, spring onions, coriander, wine, vinegar, fish sauce and sesame oil in a bowl and mix to combine. Set aside.

2 Place mussels in a large steamer, set over a saucepan of boiling water, cover and steam for 5 minutes or until mussels open. Discard any mussels that do not open after 5 minutes cooking. Spoon sauce over mussels and heat for 1 minute longer. Serve immediately.

Note: It may be necessary to steam the mussels in batches. For a complete meal serve with boiled brown or white rice and steamed vegetables of your choice.

Serves 4

443 kilojoules/104 calories per serve -
Fat low   **Fibre** low

ingredients

**1 kg/2 lb mussels, scrubbed
and beards removed**

Ginger chilli sauce
**5cm/2in piece fresh ginger,
finely chopped**
3 cloves garlic, crushed
**1 stalk lemon grass, finely chopped or
1 teaspoon dried lemon grass soaked
in hot water until soft**
3 small fresh red chillies, finely sliced
3 spring onions, diagonally sliced
4 tablespoons coriander leaves
1/4 cup/60mL/2fl oz white wine
2 tablespoons rice vinegar
1 tablespoon fish sauce
2 teaspoons sesame oil

chicken
spinach parcels

Method:

1 Place spinach in a steamer set over a saucepan of boiling water and cook for 3 minutes or until spinach wilts. Remove from steamer and cool slightly. Squeeze to remove as much moisture as possible, chop roughly and place in a bowl. Add butter, garlic and sage to spinach and mix to combine.

2 Make a deep slit in the side of each chicken fillet to form a pocket. Fill pocket with spinach mixture then secure with wooden toothpicks or cocktail sticks.

3 Wrap each fillet loosely in aluminium foil and place in a steamer set over a saucepan of boiling water. Cover and steam for 30 minutes or until chicken is tender. Remove steamer from pan, set aside and keep warm.

4 To make sauce, place stock, wine and mustard in a saucepan and bring to the boil. Reduce heat and simmer until mixture is reduced by half. Pour stock mixture into a bowl and cool for 5 minutes. Stir in yoghurt and chives and serve with chicken.

Serves 4

944 kilojoules/226 calories per serve - **Fat** low   **Fibre** medium

ingredients

I bunch English spinach
15g/¹/₂oz butter, softened
2 cloves garlic
2 tablespoons chopped fresh sage or
I teaspoon dried sage
4 boneless chicken breast fillets, skinned and trimmed of all visible fat

Creamy sauce
¹/₂ cup/125mL/4fl oz chicken stock
¹/₂ cup/125mL/4fl oz dry white wine
I tablespoon wholegrain mustard
¹/₄ cup/45g/1¹/₂oz low-fat natural yoghurt
I tablespoon snipped fresh chives

lettuce roll ups

green cuisine

Fresh vegetables are one of the

mainstays of a healthy diet, providing essential vitamins, minerals, fibre and are virtually non-existent in fat. When you tempt your tastebuds with our light, refreshing and spicy selection of vegetable and salad recipes, you can safely come back for a second helping.

lettuce
roll-ups

Photograph page 47

ingredients

6 large lettuce leaves
1 cup/60g bean sprouts
2 mangoes, peeled and chopped
260g/9oz canned sliced water chest-nuts, drained
2 teaspoons finely chopped preserved ginger
2 teaspoons finely chopped mint leaves
3 tablespoons low fat mayonnaise
1 tablespoon low fat unflavoured yoghurt

Method:
1. *Tear lettuce leaves in half lengthways. Toss together sprouts, mangoes, water chestnuts, ginger and mint.*
2. *Combine mayonnaise and yoghurt. Fold through mango mixture.*
3. *Place a spoonful of mixture on each lettuce leaf. Roll up tightly and secure with a toothpick.*

Serves 6

581 kilojoules/141 calories per serve
Fat *low*   **Fibre** *high*

french
bean salad

ingredients

500g/1 lb green beans, trimmed and sliced
1 clove garlic, crushed
1 teaspoon ground fenugreek
2 tablespoons finely chopped fresh mint leaves
1 teaspoon red wine vinegar
1 tablespoon olive oil
2 teaspoons toasted sesame seeds

Method:
1. *Boil, steam or microwave beans until just tender. Drain and place in a salad bowl.*
2. *Combine garlic, fenugreek and mint. Toss with warm beans. Set aside and allow to cool slightly.*
3. *Blend together vinegar and olive oil, pour over beans and refrigerate for 1-2 hours. Sprinkle with sesame seeds and serve.*

Serves 4

276 kilojoules/66 calories per serve
Fat *medium*   **Fibre** *high*

stir-fried
greens

Method:

1 Place sesame seeds and garlic in a nonstick frying pan and stir-fry over a medium heat for 2 minutes or until golden.

2 Add snow peas (mangetout), Chinese greens, bean sprouts, soy sauce, oyster sauce and chilli sauce to pan and stir-fry for 3 minutes or until vegetables are tender. Serve immediately.

Note: Ordinary cabbage is a suitable alternative to the Chinese greens in this recipe.

Serves 4

371 kilojoules/89 calories per serve -
Fat *low* **Fibre** *high*

ingredients

**2 tablespoons sesame seeds
1 clove garlic, crushed
185g/6oz snow peas (mangetout)
185g/6oz Chinese greens such as bok choy, Chinese broccoli and Chinese cabbage, chopped
155g/5oz bean sprouts
2 tablespoons sweet soy sauce
1 tablespoon oyster sauce
1 tablespoon sweet chilli sauce**

warm
squid salad

Method:

1 Place squid (calamari), chilli sauce, vinegar and coriander in a bowl and toss to combine. Cover and marinate at room temperature for 30 minutes or in the refrigerator overnight.

2 Drain squid (calamari) and cook on a preheated hot barbecue plate (griddle) for 2 minutes or until squid (calamari) is tender.

3 Arrange lettuce leaves, snow pea (mangetout) sprouts or watercress and tomatoes attractively on a platter, top with warm squid (calamari) and serve immediately.

Note: To clean squid (calamari), pull tentacles from the squid (calamari), carefully taking with them the stomach and ink bag. Next cut the beak, stomach and ink bag from the tentacles and discard. Wash tentacles well. Wash 'hood' and peel away skin. Cut hood in rings.

Serves 4

272 kilojoules/65 calories per serve -
Fat low   **Fibre** medium

ingredients

2 squid (calamari) tubes, cut into rings
3 tablespoons sweet chilli sauce
2 tablespoons red wine vinegar
2 tablespoons chopped fresh coriander
250g/8oz assorted lettuce leaves
125g/4oz snow pea (mangetout) sprouts
or watercress
250g/8oz cherry tomatoes, halved

spaghetti
with asparagus sauce

Method:

1 Cook spaghetti in boiling water in a large saucepan following packet directions.

2 To make sauce, steam, boil or microwave asparagus until tender. Drain and refresh under cold running water. Cut into 3cm/1¼in pieces and set aside. Heat oil in a frypan, add breadcrumbs and cook over low heat for 2 minutes, stirring all the time. Stir in milk and asparagus, and cook over medium heat for 5 minutes. Mix in cheese and continue to cook until melted. Season to taste with pepper.

3 Place spaghetti on a warmed serving platter, spoon over sauce and toss gently to combine. Sprinkle with Parmesan cheese and serve immediately.

Serves 6

1000 kilojoules/237 calories per serve
Fat medium   **Fibre** medium

ingredients

500g/1lb spaghetti
2 tablespoons grated Parmesan cheese

Asparagus sauce
500g/1lb fresh asparagus spears, trimmed
1 tablespoon olive oil
1 thick slice wholegrain bread, crumbed
1 cup/250mL evaporated skim milk
60g/2oz grated mozzarella cheese
freshly ground black pepper

stir-fried
broccoli with almonds

Method:

1 Boil, steam or microwave carrots and broccoli until they just change colour. Drain and refresh under cold running water.

2 Heat oil in wok or frypan. Add onion, garlic and ginger and stir-fry for 4-5 minutes. Add carrots, broccoli and soy sauce, and stir-fry for 3-4 minutes longer, or until vegetables are heated through. Just prior to serving toss through almonds.

Serves 4

390 kilojoules/92 calories per serve
Fat low   **Fibre** high

ingredients

2 carrots, cut into matchsticks
500g/1 lb broccoli, cut into florets
2 teaspoons peanut oil
1 onion, sliced
1 clove garlic, crushed
2 teaspoons grated fresh ginger
2 teaspoons low salt soy sauce
2 tablespoons toasted almonds

mixed
pepper and onion tart

Method:

1. Place stock and brown sugar in a nonstick frying pan and cook over a medium heat for 3-4 minutes or until sugar dissolves. Add onions and cook, stirring, for 15 minutes or until onions start to caramelise.

2. Layer pastry sheets, brushing between each layer with water. Brush top sheet of pastry with oil and use layered pastry to line a lightly greased 18x28cm/7x11in shallow cake tin. Roll pastry edges to neaten.

3. Place ricotta cheese, basil and black pepper to taste in a bowl and mix to combine. Spread ricotta mixture over pastry, then top with onions and roasted capsicums (peppers) and bake for 20 minutes or until pastry is crisp and golden.

Serves 6

655 kilojoules/156 calories per serve –
Fat *low*   **Fibre** *low*

ingredients

$^1/_4$ **cup/60mL/2fl oz chicken stock**
2 teaspoons brown sugar
3 onions, thinly sliced
8 sheets filo pastry
$^1/_4$ **cup/60mL/2fl oz water**
1 tablespoon oil
200g/6$^1/_2$oz ricotta cheese, drained
2 tablespoons chopped fresh basil
freshly ground black pepper
**1 red capsicum (pepper), roasted
and cut into thin strips**
**1 green capsicum (pepper), roasted
and cut into thin strips**

Oven temperature 180°C, 350°F, Gas 4

herby
vegetable salad

Method:

1 Boil, steam or microwave cauliflower, broccoli, carrot and snow peas (mangetout) until just tender. Drain, refresh under cold water.
2 Drain vegetables well. Toss in a salad bowl with capsicum (pepper), lemon juice, cilantra (coriander) and rosemary. Season to taste with pepper. Refrigerate until required.
3 To make vinaigrette, combine all ingredients in a screwtop jar. Shake well to combine. Pour over salad just prior to serving.

Serves 4

348 kilojoules/82 calories per serve
Fat low   **Fibre** medium

ingredients

¹/₄ **cauliflower, broken into florets**
1 head broccoli, broken into florets
1 large carrot, cut into thin strips
150g/5oz snow peas (mangetout), trimmed
1 red capsicum (pepper), cut into thin strips
3 tablespoons lemon juice
2 teaspoons finely chopped fresh cilantra (coriander)
2 teaspoons finely chopped fresh rosemary
freshly ground black pepper

Lemon Viniagrette
2 tablespoons lemon juice
1 tablespoon olive oil
1 clove garlic, crushed
1 teaspoon wholegrain mustard

spinach
and salmon timbales

Method:

1 *Boil, steam or microwave spinach until just wilted. Drain and allow to cool.*

2 *Select the largest spinach leaves and use to line four very lightly greased individual ramekins of about 1 cup/250mL capacity. Leave some of the leaves overhanging the top.*

3 *To make filling, squeeze as much liquid as possible from remaining spinach and chop finely. In a food processor or blender, combine salmon, ricotta, chives, parsley and egg. Process until smooth. Mix in chopped spinach and season with pepper.*

4 *Spoon mixture into prepared ramekins. Fold spinach leaves over the top. Bake at 180°C/350°C/Gas 4 for 30 minutes or until set.*

Serves 4

652 kilojoules/156 calories per serve
Fat *low*   **Fibre** *high*

ingredients

**1 bunch English spinach
(about 1 kg/2lb), washed**

Filling
220g/7oz canned salmon, drained
100g/3 1/2oz ricotta cheese
2 tablespoon finely chopped chives
2 tablespoons finely chopped fresh parsley
1 egg, lightly beaten
freshly ground black pepper

Oven temperature 180°C, 350°F, Gas 4

cajun chicken with
pawpaw salsa

dinner winners

This tasty selection of dinner menus

for everyday family meals will fit into your eating
plan and leave the rest of the family feeling satisfied
and healthy.

cajun
chicken with pawpaw salsa

Photograph page 57

Oven temperature 180°C, 350°F, Gas 4

Method:

1 Rub chicken with crushed garlic. Place onion salt, white pepper, black pepper, cayenne pepper, paprika and mixed herbs in a bowl and mix to combine.

2 Rub spice mixture over chicken, place on a nonstick baking tray and bake for 25-30 minutes or until chicken is tender. Cover and stand for 5 minutes before serving.

3 To make salsa, place pawpaw, cucumber, mint, yoghurt and lime juice in a bowl and mix to combine. Serve with chicken.

Note: After rubbing spice mixture onto chicken wash your hands and do not touch your face or lips as the cayenne pepper causes burning.

Serves 4

933 kilojoules/223 calories per serve –
Fat *low* **Fibre** *medium*

ingredients

4 boneless chicken breast fillets, skinned and trimmed of all visible fat
2 cloves garlic, crushed
1 tablespoon onion salt
1 tablespoon ground white pepper
1 tablespoon cracked black pepper
2 teaspoons cayenne pepper
1 tablespoon paprika
1 tablespoon dried mixed herbs

Pawpaw salsa
1 small pawpaw, diced
1 cucumber, diced
2 tablespoons mint leaves
2 tablespoons low-fat natural yoghurt
2 tablespoons lime juice

pasta
with goat's cheese

Method:

1 Cook pasta in boiling water in a saucepan following packet directions. Drain, set aside and keep warm.

2 Heat oil in a nonstick frying pan over a medium heat, add garlic and cook, stirring, for 2 minutes or until golden. Add breadcrumbs and cook, stirring, for 5 minutes or until breadcrumbs are crisp and golden. Remove from pan and set aside.

3 Add tomatoes and rocket to pan and cook, stirring occasionally, for 5 minutes or until tomatoes are soft and rocket wilts. Add tomato mixture, breadcrumb mixture and cheese to pasta and toss to combine.

Serves 4

933 kilojoules/223 calories per serve –
Fat *low* **Fibre** *medium*

ingredients

500g/1 lb tagliatelle
2 teaspoons olive oil
2 cloves garlic, crushed
1 cup/60g/2oz wholemeal breadcrumbs, made from stale bread
250g/8oz cherry tomatoes, halved
1 bunch rocket
90g/3oz goat's cheese

spicy
seafood stir-fry

Method:

1 Make a single cut down length of each squid (calamari) tube and open out. Using a sharp knife, cut parallel lines down the length of the squid (calamari), taking care not to cut right through the flesh. Make more cuts in the opposite direction to form a diamond pattern. Cut each piece into 2¹/₂cm/1in squares. Set aside.

2 Heat oil in a wok or frying pan over a high heat, add onion, ginger, garlic and chilli paste (sambal oelek) and stir-fry for 2 minutes or until onion is golden. Add red capsicum (pepper), yellow capsicum (pepper), lime juice and honey and stir-fry for 2 minutes longer.

3 Add squid (calamari), prawns (shrimp) and scallops and stir-fry for 5 minutes or until prawns just change colour. Add beans, snow peas (mangetout) and coconut milk and cook for 2 minutes or until seafood is cooked.

Serves 4

1219 kilojoules/291 calories per serve - **Fat** *low* **Fibre** *medium*

ingredients

2 squid (calamari) tubes (bodies)
1 tablespoon sesame oil
1 onion, cut into wedges and layers separated
2 teaspoons finely chopped fresh ginger
1 clove garlic, crushed
2 teaspoons chilli paste (sambal oelek)
1 red capsicum (pepper), chopped
1 yellow capsicum (pepper), chopped
2 tablespoons lime juice
1 tablespoon honey
315g/10oz medium uncooked prawns (shrimp), shelled and deveined
90g/3oz scallops, cleaned
125g/4oz green beans, cut into 2¹/₂cm/1in pieces
125g/4oz snow peas (mangetout)
¹/₄ cup/60mL/2fl oz coconut milk

pumpkin
and artichoke risotto

Method:

1 Place stock and wine in a saucepan and bring to the boil over a medium heat. Reduce heat and keep warm.

2 Heat oil in a saucepan over a medium heat, add onion, cumin and nutmeg and cook, stirring, for 3 minutes or until onion is soft. Add pumpkin and cook, stirring, for 3 minutes.

3 Add rice and cook, stirring, for 5 minutes. Pour 1 cup/250mL/8fl oz hot stock mixture into rice and cook over a medium heat, stirring constantly, until stock is absorbed. Continue cooking in this way until all the stock is used and rice is tender.

4 Add artichokes, sun-dried tomatoes, sage and black pepper to taste to rice mixture. Mix gently and cook for 2 minutes or until heated through. Remove pan from heat, gently stir in Parmesan cheese and serve.

Note: Arborio or risotto rice is traditionally used for making risottos. It absorbs liquid without becoming soft and it is this special quality that makes it so suitable for risottos. A risotto made in the traditional way, where liquid is added gradually as the rice cooks, takes 20-30 minutes to cook.

Serves 4

2037 kilojoules/487 calories per serve - **Fat** *low* **Fibre** *high*

ingredients

3 cups/750mL/1¼pt vegetable stock
1 cup/250 mL/8fl oz white wine
1 tablespoon olive oil
1 onion, chopped
2 teaspoons ground cumin
½ teaspoon nutmeg
185g/6oz pumpkin, chopped
1½ cups/330g/10½ oz Arborio
or risotto rice
440g/14oz canned artichoke hearts,
drained and chopped
90g/3oz sun-dried tomatoes, chopped
2 tablespoons chopped fresh sage
freshly ground black pepper
30g/1oz grated Parmesan cheese

fish
and chippies

Method:

1 *Pat fish dry with absorbent kitchen paper and set aside.*

2 *Place garlic, dill, wine and lemon juice in a shallow glass or ceramic dish and mix to combine. Add fish, cover and marinate in the refrigerator for 2 hours.*

3 *Place potatoes on a nonstick baking tray, brush lightly with oil and bake, turning several times, for 30-45 minutes or until potatoes are crisp and golden.*

4 *Drain fish well and cook under a preheated medium grill for 5 minutes or until fish flakes when tested with a fork. Serve immediately with potato wedges.*

Serves 4

1449 kilojoules/346 calories per serve –
Fat *low*   **Fibre** *high*

ingredients

**4 firm white fish fillets
1 clove garlic, crushed
1 tablespoon chopped fresh dill
1/4 cup/60mL/2fl oz white wine
2 tablespoons lemon juice
4 large potatoes, cut into wedges
1 tablespoon olive oil**

Oven temperature 220°C, 425°F, Gas 7

pork
with mango couscous

Photograph page 62

ingredients

1¹/₂ kg/3 lb boneless pork loin, rind removed
and trimmed of all visible fat

Mango couscous stuffing
¹/₂ cup/90g/3oz couscous
¹/₂ cup/125mL/4fl oz boiling water
¹/₂ mango, chopped
2 spring onions, chopped
3 tablespoons chopped fresh cilantra (coriander)
2 teaspoons finely grated lime rind
¹/₂ teaspoon garam masala
1 egg white, lightly beaten
1 tablespoon lime juice

Creamy wine sauce
¹/₂ cup/125mL/4fl oz chicken stock
¹/₂ cup/125mL/4fl oz white wine
2 tablespoons low-fat natural yoghurt

pork with mango couscous

Method:

1 To make stuffing, place couscous in a bowl, pour over boiling water and toss with a fork until couscous absorbs all the liquid. Add mango, spring onions, cilantra (coriander), lime rind, garam masala, egg white and lime juice and mix to combine.

2 Lay pork out flat and spread stuffing evenly over surface. Roll up firmly and secure with string. Place pork on a wire rack set in a roasting tin, pour in 2¹/₂cm/1in water and bake for 1¹/₂ hours or until pork is cooked to your liking. Place pork on a serving platter, set aside and keep warm.

3 To make sauce, skim excess fat from pan juices, stir in stock and wine and bring to the boil over a medium heat. Reduce heat and simmer for 10 minutes or until sauce reduces by half. Remove tin from heat and whisk in yoghurt. Slice pork and serve with sauce.

Note: On completion of cooking, remove meat from oven, cover and stand in a warm place for 10-15 minutes before carving. Standing allows the juices to settle and makes carving easier.

Serves 8

1471 kilojoules/351 calories per serve -
Fat *medium*   **Fibre** *low*

red
wine steaks

Method:

1. To make marinade, place wine, Worcestershire sauce, mustard and black pepper to taste in a shallow dish and mix to combine.
2. Add steaks to marinade and set aside to marinate for at least 30 minutes. Cook steaks on a preheated hot barbecue or under a grill for 3-5 minutes each side or until cooked to your liking.

Serves 4

1105 kilojoules/264 calories per serve - **Fat** medium **Fibre** low

ingredients

4 lean boneless sirloin steaks

Red wine marinade
1/4 **cup/60mL/2fl oz red wine**
2 **tablespoons Worcestershire sauce**
2 **teaspoons French mustard**
freshly ground black pepper

spicy
marinated lamb kebabs

Method:

1 To make marinade, combine honey, soy, garlic, cinnamon and sesame oil in a glass bowl. Add meat and marinate for 30 minutes.

2 Remove meat from marinade and thread meat onto eight bamboo skewers, alternating with capsicum (pepper), mushrooms and courgettes (zucchini). Grill under medium heat for 8-10 minutes, turning frequently and basting with marinade.

Serves 4

1415 kilojoules/339 calories per serve
Fat *medium*   **Fibre** *medium*

ingredients

500g/1lb lean lamb, cubed
1 large green capsicum (pepper), cubed
16 button mushrooms
**2 medium courgettes (zucchini),
sliced into 2cm/³/₄in widths**

Marinade
2 tablespoons honey
1 tablespoon low-salt soy sauce
1 clove garlic, crushed
¹/₂ teaspoon ground cinnamon
2 teaspoons sesame oil

herbed
ham and pineapple pizza

Method:

1 To make dough, place sugar, yeast and
$^1/_4$ cup/60mL/2fl oz water in a bowl and whisk
with a fork until yeast dissolves. Set aside in
a warm draught-free place for 5 minutes or
until mixture is foamy.

2 Sift wholemeal flour and flour together into a
bowl. Return husks to bowl. Stir in oil, yeast
mixture and remaining water and mix to
make a soft dough. Turn onto a lightly
floured surface and knead for 10 minutes or
until dough is smooth and glossy.

3 Place dough in a lightly oiled bowl, cover
with plastic food wrap and set aside in a
warm draught-free place for 1 hour or until
doubled in volume. Punch dough down and
divide into two equal portions.

4 On a lightly floured surface roll out dough
to form two 30cm/12in rounds. Place pizza
bases on lightly greased baking trays and
spread with tomato paste (purée).
Then spread with pasta sauce and top with
pineapple pieces, ham and red capsicum
(pepper). Sprinkle with spring onions, cheese
and parsley and bake for 20 minutes or until
bases are crisp and cooked.

Serves 8

1403 kilojoules/335 calories per serve -
Fat *low* **Fibre** *high*

ingredients

Wholemeal pizza dough
3 teaspoons sugar
7g/$^1/_4$oz active dry yeast
1 cup/250mL/8fl oz warm water
2 cups/315g/10oz wholemeal flour
1$^1/_4$ cups/155g/5oz flour
$^1/_4$ cup/60mL/2fl oz vegetable oil

Ham and pineapple topping
2 tablespoons tomato paste (purée)
1 cup/250mL/8fl oz bottled
tomato pasta sauce
440g/14oz canned pineapple pieces
in natural juices, drained
125g/4oz lean ham, chopped
1 red capsicum (pepper), sliced
4 spring onions, chopped
60g/2oz reduced-fat grated
mozzarella cheese
2 tablespoons chopped fresh parsley

Oven temperature 220°C, 425°F, Gas 7

lamb
with roast capsicum (pepper) purée

Method:

1 Place garlic, wine, vinegar, mustard and honey in a shallow glass or ceramic dish and mix to combine. Add lamb, cover and marinate in the refrigerator for 3-4 hours or overnight.

2 To make purée, place red and yellow capsicum (peppers), skin side up, under a preheated hot grill and cook for 10-15 minutes or until skins are blistered and charred. Place peppers in a plastic food bag or paper bag and set aside until cool enough to handle, then remove skins. Place capsicum (peppers) and yoghurt in a food processor or blender and process to make a purée. Stir in mint and set aside.

3 Drain lamb and cook under a preheated medium grill or on a barbecue for 3-5 minutes each side or until lamb is cooked to your liking. Serve with purée.

Serves 4

1232 kilojoules/294 calories per serve -
Fat *medium* **Fibre** *low*

ingredients

1 clove garlic, crushed
¼ cup/60mL/2fl oz white wine
2 tablespoons tarragon vinegar
2 tablespoons wholegrain mustard
1 tablespoon honey
8 lamb cutlets, trimmed of all visible fat

Roast capsicum (pepper) purée
1 red capsicum (pepper), seeded and quartered
1 yellow capsicum (pepper), seeded and quartered
½ cup/100g/3½oz low-fat yoghurt
2 tablespoons chopped fresh mint

orange
chicken

Photograph page 69

ingredients

4 boneless chicken breasts, skinned
2 teaspoons cornflour blended with
3 tablespoons chicken stock

Marinade
³/₄ cup/190mL orange juice
1 tablespoon grated orange rind
¹/₂ teaspoon French mustard
¹/₂ teaspoon ground nutmeg
¹/₂ teaspoon curry powder
freshly ground black pepper

Method:

1 *To make marinade, combine orange juice, rind, mustard, nutmeg and curry powder in a shallow glass dish. Season to taste with pepper. Add chicken and marinate for 1-2 hours.*

2 *Transfer chicken and a little of the marinade to a baking dish. Bake at 180°C/350°C/Gas 4 for 30 minutes or until chicken is tender. Place remaining marinade and cornflour mixture in a saucepan. Cook over medium heat until sauce boils and thickens. Spoon over chicken and serve.*

Serves 4

893 kilojoules/215 calories per serve
Fat *low* **Fibre** *low*

Oven temperature 180°C, 350°F, Gas 4

pork
with prunes and apricots

Photograph page 69

ingredients

2 tablespoons polyunsaturated oil
500g/1lb lean pork, cubed
1 onion, cut into eighths
¹/₂ teaspoon ground sage
¹/₂ teaspoon ground thyme
1 cup/250mL apple juice
10 large pitted prunes
1 teaspoon cider vinegar
8 dried apricots
2 tablespoons slivered almonds, toasted

Method:

1 *Heat oil in a frypan. Cook pork, onion, sage and thyme until meat changes colour and is just tender.*

2 *Puree apple juice, six prunes and vinegar in a food processor or blender and pour onto meat in pan. Stir in apricots and remaining prunes. Cook, covered, for 15 minutes, stirring occasionally. Serve sprinkled with almonds.*

Serves 4

1123 kilojoules/269 calories per serve
Fat *low* **Fibre** *high*

Oven temperature 180°C, 350°F, Gas 4

sweet
treats

tropical rice pudding

sweet
treats

Our light, luscious and refreshing

*Our light, luscious and refreshing selection of dessert
recipes will satisfy any cravings for something sweet
and keep you slim and healthy.*

berry
peach parfaits

Method:

1 Place ricotta cheese, yoghurt, maple syrup and liqueur in a bowl and beat until smooth.
2 Place a layer of ricotta mixture into the base of a parfait glass, top with a layer of mixed berries, then a second layer of ricotta mixture, a layer of peaches and a final layer of ricotta mixture. Decorate with strawberries and coconut. Repeat with remaining fruit and ricotta mixture to make six desserts.

Serves 6

906 kilojoules/216 calories per serve - **Fat** low **Fibre** high

ingredients

200g/6¹/₂oz ricotta cheese
1 cup/200g/6¹/₂oz low-fat natural yoghurt
¹/₄ cup/60mL/2fl oz maple syrup
1 tablespoon orange-flavoured liqueur
500g/1 lb mixed berries of your choice, such as blueberries and raspberries or strawberries and blackberries
440g/14oz canned peach slices in natural juice, drained
6 strawberries, halved
¹/₂ cup/45g/1¹/₂oz shredded coconut, toasted

tropical
rice pudding

Photograph page 71

Method:

1 Place rice, reduced-fat milk, coconut milk, orange rind, cinnamon stick and vanilla bean (pod) in a saucepan and bring to the boil. Reduce heat, cover and simmer over a low heat for 15 minutes or until rice is tender and liquid is absorbed. Remove pan from heat, discard cinnamon stick and vanilla bean (pod) and cool slightly.
2 Stir brown sugar, egg yolks and rum into rice mixture and mix well.
3 Place egg whites in a clean bowl and beat until stiff peaks form. Fold egg whites into rice mixture. Spoon mixture in a lightly greased 23cm/9in fluted ring tin. Place ring tin in a baking dish, add enough hot water to come halfway up the sides of the tin and bake for 40 minutes or until set.
4 Remove tin from baking dish and set aside to cool. Turn mould onto a serving dish, fill centre with fruit and drizzle mould and fruit with passion fruit pulp.

Serves 8

1311 kilojoules/313 calories per serve - **Fat** low **Fibre** medium

ingredients

1 cup/220g/7oz basmati rice
2¹/₂ cups/600 mL/1pt reduced-fat milk
¹/₂ cup/125mL/4fl oz coconut milk
1 tablespoon finely grated orange rind
1 cinnamon stick
1 vanilla bean (pod), split
1 cup/170g/5¹/₂oz brown sugar
3 eggs, separated
2 tablespoons dark rum
500g/1 lb tropical fruit of your choice, such as sliced guavas, tamarillos, kiwifruit, starfruit, mangoes, pawpaw and pineapple
6 passion fruit

Oven temperature 190°C, 375°F, Gas 5

raspberry
and yoghurt mousse

Method:

1 Place raspberries in a food processor or blender and process to make a purée. Press purée through a sieve to remove seeds. Stir in icing sugar.

2 Place ricotta cheese, yoghurt, sugar, vanilla essence and lime or lemon juice in a food processor or blender and process until smooth.

3 Divide mixture into two equal portions. Stir raspberry purée into one portion. Alternate spoonfuls of plain and raspberry mixtures in serving glasses and swirl to give a ripple pattern. Refrigerate for at least 1 hour.

Note: To make thick yogurt, line a sieve with a double thickness of muslin or absorbent kitchen paper and place over a bowl. Place yogurt in sieve and set aside to drain for 2-3 hours at room temperature or overnight in the refrigerator.

Serves 6

647 kilojoules/155 calories per serve -
Fat *medium*   **Fibre** *medium*

ingredients

315g/10oz fresh or frozen raspberries
2 teaspoons icing sugar
350g/11oz ricotta cheese
1 cup/200g/6¹/₂oz thick low-fat natural yoghurt
2 tablespoons caster sugar
2 teaspoons vanilla essence
2 teaspoons lime or lemon juice

passion fruit
souffle

Method:

1 *Place ricotta cheese, passion fruit pulp, egg yolks, liqueur and half the caster sugar in a bowl and beat for 5 minutes or until mixture is smooth.*

2 *Place egg whites and cream of tartar in a clean bowl and beat until soft peaks form. Gradually beat in remaining caster sugar until stiff peaks form.*

3 *Fold one-third egg white mixture into passion fruit mixture, then fold in remaining egg white mixture.*

4 *Pour soufflé mixture into a greased 20cm /8in soufflé dish and bake for 20 minutes or until soufflé is well risen. Sprinkle with icing sugar and serve.*

Serves 4-6

701 kilojoules/167 calories per serve -
Fat *low*   **Fibre** *high*

ingredients

60g/2oz ricotta cheese
1¹/₂ cups/375mL/12fl oz passion fruit pulp
2 egg yolks
1 tablespoon orange-flavoured liqueur
¹/₃ cup/75g/2¹/₂oz caster sugar
6 egg whites
pinch cream of tartar
icing sugar, sifted

Oven temperature 180°C, 350°F, Gas 4

apple
and date ricotta slice

Method:

1. Place flour and butter in a food processor and process until mixture resembles fine breadcrumbs. Add sugar and process to combine. With machine running, slowly add enough water to form a rough dough. Turn dough onto a lightly floured surface and knead briefly. Wrap dough in plastic food wrap and refrigerate for 20 minutes.
2. Roll out dough to 5mm/¼in thick and large enough to line the base of a lightly greased and lined 23cm/9in square cake tin.
3. For topping, arrange apples and dates over pastry.
4. Place ricotta cheese, sugar, flour, milk, eggs and brandy in a bowl and beat until smooth. Spoon ricotta mixture over fruit, spread out evenly and bake for 1 hour or until topping is set. Cool in tin, then cut into squares.

Makes 36

384 kilojoules/92 calories per serve - low fibre; low fat

ingredients

1½ cups/235g/7½oz wholemeal self-raising flour
60g/2oz butter or margarine
½ cup/100g/3½oz caster sugar
¼-⅓ cup/60-90mL/2-3fl oz iced water

Apple date topping
440g/14oz canned pie apple, drained
90g/3oz fresh or dried dates, pitted and halved
500g/1 lb ricotta cheese, drained
½ cup/100g/3½oz caster sugar
2 tablespoons flour
½ cup/125mL/4fl oz reduced-fat milk
2 eggs, lightly beaten
1 tablespoon brandy

creamy
cheesecake

Method:

1 To make base, combine biscuit crumbs, nuts and butter. Spread over the base of a lightly greased 20cm/8in springform pan and set aside.

2 To make filling, place ricotta, cottage cheese, semolina, buttermilk and egg yolks in a food processor or blender and process until smooth.

3 Beat egg whites until soft peaks form. Add sugar a spoonful at a time, beating well after each addition until whites are thick and glossy.

4 Fold cheese mixture into egg whites, then lightly fold through lemon rind and sultanas. Spoon mixture into prepared pan and bake at 180°C/350°F/Gas 4 for 50-55 minutes or until firm. Cool in pan.

Serves 8

1399 kilojoules/334 calories per serve
Fat medium   **Fibre** low

ingredients

Base
125g/4oz sweet biscuit crumbs
1 tablespoon ground hazelnuts
60g/2oz butter, melted

Filling
250g/8oz ricotta cheese
125g/4oz cottage cheese
1 tablespoon fine semolina
2 tablespoons buttermilk
3 eggs, separated
³/₄ cup/190g/6oz caster sugar
2 teaspoons grated lemon rind
3 tablespoons sultanas

Oven temperature 180°C, 350°F, Gas 4

Oven temperature 200°C, 400°F, Gas 6

fruit
brulee

Method:

1 Place apple, sultanas and cinnamon in a bowl and mix to combine. Divide mixture between four 1 cup/250mL/8fl oz capacity ramekins.

2 To make topping, place yoghurt, ricotta cheese and vanilla essence in a food processor or blender and process until smooth. Spread topping over fruit, sprinkle with sugar and bake for 25 minutes or until fruit is heated through and top is golden.

Serves 4

661 kilojoules/158 calories per serve -
Fat *low* ***Fibre*** *medium*

ingredients

440g/14oz canned unsweetened apple pie filling
4 tablespoons sultanas
1 teaspoon ground cinnamon

Yoghurt topping
¹/₂ cup/100g/3¹/₂oz low-fat natural yoghurt
¹/₂ cup/125g/4oz ricotta cheese
1 teaspoon vanilla essence
1¹/₂ tablespoons brown sugar

Cooking is not an exact science: one does not require finely calibrated scales, pipettes and scientific equipment to cook, yet the conversion to metric measures in some countries and its interpretations must have intimidated many a good cook.

Weights are given in the recipes only for ingredients such as meats, fish, poultry and some vegetables. Though a few grams/ounces one way or another will not affect the success of your dish.

Though recipes have been tested using the Australian Standard 250mL cup, 20mL tablespoon and 5mL teaspoon, they will work just as well with the US and Canadian 8fl oz cup, or the UK 300mL cup. We have used graduated cup measures in preference to tablespoon measures so that proportions are always the same. Where tablespoon measures have been given, these are not crucial measures, so using the smaller tablespoon of the US or UK will not affect the recipe's success. At least we all agree on the teaspoon size.

For breads, cakes and pastries, the only area which might cause concern is where eggs are used, as proportions will then vary. If working with a 250mL or 300mL cup, use large eggs (60g/2oz), adding a little more liquid to the recipe for 300mL cup measures if it seems necessary. Use the medium-sized eggs (55g/1¼oz) with 8fl oz cup measure. A graduated set of measuring cups and spoons is recommended, the cups in particular for measuring dry ingredients. Remember to level such ingredients to ensure their accuracy.

English measures

All measurements are similar to Australian with two exceptions: the English cup measures 300mL/10fl oz, whereas the Australian cup measure 250mL/8fl oz. The English tablespoon (the Australian dessertspoon) measures 14.8mL/½fl oz against the Australian tablespoon of 20mL/¾fl oz.

American measures

The American reputed pint is 16fl oz, a quart is equal to 32fl oz and the American gallon, 128fl oz. The Imperial measurement is 20fl oz to the pint, 40fl oz a quart and 160fl oz one gallon.

The American tablespoon is equal to 14.8mL/½fl oz, the teaspoon is 5mL/⅙fl oz. The cup measure is 250mL/8fl oz, the same as Australia.

Dry measures

All the measures are level, so when you have filled a cup or spoon, level it off with the edge of a knife. The scale below is the "cook's equivalent"; it is not an exact conversion of metric to imperial measurement. To calculate the exact metric equivalent yourself, use 2.2046 lb = 1kg or 1 lb = 0.45359kg

Metric		Imperial	
g = grams		oz = ounces	
kg = kilograms		lb = pound	
15g		½oz	
20g		⅔oz	
30g		1oz	
60g		2oz	
90g		3oz	
125g		4oz	¼ lb
155g		5oz	
185g		6oz	
220g		7oz	
250g		8oz	½ lb
280g		9oz	
315g		10oz	
345g		11oz	
375g		12oz	¾ lb
410g		13oz	
440g		14oz	
470g		15oz	
1,000g	1kg	35.2oz	2.2 lb
	1.5kg		3.3 lb

Oven temperatures

The Celsius temperatures given here are not exact; they have been rounded off and are given as a guide only. Follow the manufacturer's temperature guide, relating it to oven description given in the recipe. Remember gas ovens are hottest at the top, electric ovens at the bottom and convection-fan forced ovens are usually even throughout. We included Regulo numbers for gas cookers which may assist. To convert °C to °F multiply °C by 9 and divide by 5 then add 32.

Oven temperatures

	C°	F°	Regulo
Very slow	120	250	1
Slow	150	300	2
Moderately slow	150	325	3
Moderate	180	350	4
Moderately hot	190-200	370-400	5-6
Hot	210-220	410-440	6-7
Very hot	230	450	8
Super hot	250-290	475-500	9-10

Cake dish sizes

Metric	Imperial
15cm	6in
18cm	7in
20cm	8in
23cm	9in

Loaf dish sizes

Metric	Imperial
23x12cm	9x5in
25x8cm	10x3in
28x18cm	11x7in

Liquid measures

Metric	Imperial	Cup & Spoon
mL	fl oz	
millilitres	fluid ounce	
5mL	$^1/_6$fl oz	1 teaspoon
20mL	$^2/_3$fl oz	1 tablespoon
30mL	1fl oz	1 tablespoon plus 2 teaspoons
60mL	2fl oz	$^1/_4$ cup
85mL	2$^1/_2$fl oz	$^1/_3$ cup
100mL	3fl oz	$^3/_8$ cup
125mL	4fl oz	$^1/_2$ cup
150mL	5fl oz	$^1/_4$ pint, 1 gill
250mL	8fl oz	1 cup
300mL	10fl oz	$^1/_2$ pint)
360mL	12fl oz	1$^1/_2$ cups
420mL	14fl oz	1$^3/_4$ cups
500mL	16fl oz	2 cups
600mL	20fl oz 1 pint,	2$^1/_2$ cups
1 litre	35fl oz 1$^3/_4$ pints,	4 cups

Cup measurements

One cup is equal to the following weights.

	Metric	Imperial
Almonds, flaked	90g	3oz
Almonds, slivered, ground	125g	4oz
Almonds, kernel	155g	5oz
Apples, dried, chopped	125g	4oz
Apricots, dried, chopped	190g	6oz
Breadcrumbs, packet	125g	4oz

	Metric	Imperial
Breadcrumbs, soft	60g	2oz
Cheese, grated	125g	4oz
Choc bits	155g	5oz
Coconut, desiccated	90g	3oz
Cornflakes	30g	1oz
Currants	155g	5oz
Flour	125g	4oz
Fruit, dried (mixed, sultanas etc)	185g	6oz
Ginger, crystallised, glace	250g	8oz
Honey, treacle, golden syrup	315g	10oz
Mixed peel	220g	7oz
Nuts, chopped	125g	4oz
Prunes, chopped	220g	7oz
Rice, cooked	155g	5oz
Rice, uncooked	220g	7oz
Rolled oats	90g	3oz
Sesame seeds	125g	4oz
Shortening (butter, margarine)	250g	8oz
Sugar, brown	155g	5oz
Sugar, granulated or caster	250g	8oz
Sugar, sifted icing	155g	5oz
Wheatgerm	60g	2oz

Length

Some of us still have trouble converting imperial length to metric. In this scale, measures have been rounded off to the easiest-to-use and most acceptable figures.

To obtain the exact metric equivalent in converting inches to centimetres, multiply inches by 2.54 whereby 1 inch equals 25.4 millimetres and 1 millimetre equals 0.03937 inches.

Metric	Imperial
mm = millimetres	in = inches
cm = centimetres	ft = feet
5mm, 0.5cm	$^1/_4$in
10mm, 1.0cm	$^1/_2$in
20mm, 2.0cm	$^3/_4$in
2.5cm	1in
5cm	2in
8cm	3in
10cm	4in
12cm	5in
15cm	6in
18cm	7in
20cm	8in
23cm	9in
25cm	10in
28cm	11in
30cm	1 ft, 12in

index